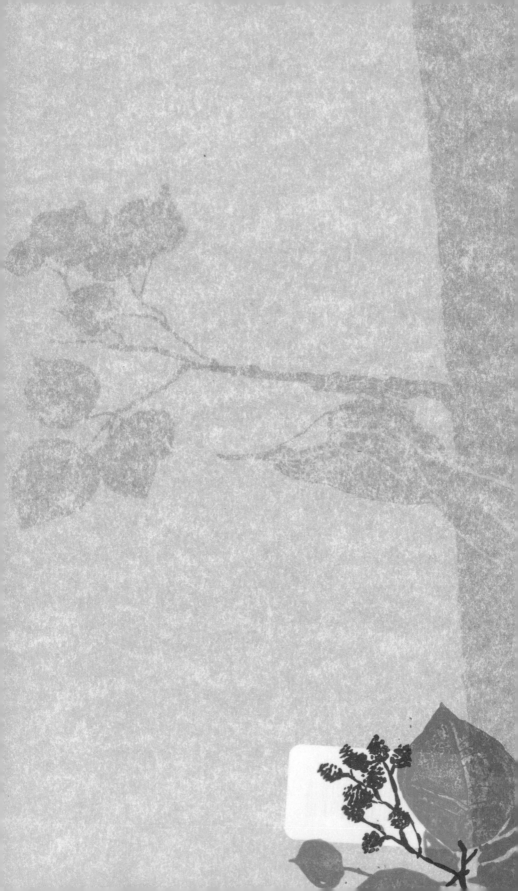

This book was designed and illustrated by Fred Klemushin.
The artist made his own color separations and closely
supervised the printing for utmost accuracy of reproduction.
The type is set in Optima, a roman typeface
of graceful simplicity designed by Hermann Zapf.
The paper is Hallclear, White Imitation Parchment and Ivory
Fiesta Parchment. The cover is bound
with natural weave book cloth and Torino paper.

….and become a shadow….

….of God's Shadow.

He who can experience....

see....

....and understand these things

can reach perfection....

....a poor man
trapped between his bitterness
and his submission....
....a rich man
between his greed
and his conscience....
....a poet
between the mist of his twilight
and the rays of his dawn....

....a worshipper in his temple....

....a criminal in his prison....

....a scholar
   amidst his parchments....

....an ignorant soul
stumbling between the darkness
   of his night
      and the obscurity
         of his day....

....a nun suffering between the
flowers of her faith
   and the thistles of her loneliness....

To attain his goal

man must perceive that....

....he is a child

dependent upon his mother....

....a father

responsible for his family....

....a youth lost in love

....an ancient

wrestling against his past....

Be like the bee....

and do not waste your spring days

....gazing on the doings

of the eagle.

Be like the child

rejoicing at the firelight....

....and let the mother abide.

All that you see was....

and still is....

....yours.

Go into your neighbor's house
and see the infant child
        bewitched by the firelight....
while the mother is busied
        at her tasks.

....but go instead into the field
and see how the bee hovers
over the sweet flowers
....and the eagle swoops down
on its prey.

Some men would see the world
with the eyes of God....
　　　　....and would grasp the secrets
of the hereafter
　　　　　　by means of human thought....

....tears with which I join

the brokenhearted....

....laughter that symbolizes joy

over my very existence.

It is my fervent hope
that my whole life on this earth
will ever be....
....tears and laughter.
....tears that purify my heart
and reveal to me
the secret of life....
....and its mystery....
....laughter that brings me
closer
to my fellow men....

I would not exchange
the laughter of my heart....
....for the fortunes
of the multitude....
....nor would I be content
with converting my tears....
....invited by my agonized self....
....into calm.

Know your own true worth
....and you shall not perish.
Reason is your light
and your beacon
of Truth.
Reason is the source
of Life.

....for Reason is a prudent minister
....a loyal guide
....and a wise counselor.
Reason is light in darkness....
as anger is darkness amidst light.

When Reason speaks to you,
hearken to what she says....
        ....and you shall be saved.
    Make good use of her utterances....
....and you shall be
        as one armed....

As the first glance

from the eyes of the beloved

is like a seed....

        ....sown in the human heart....

       ....and the first kiss of her lips

like a flower

    upon the branch

       of the Tree of Life....

     ....so the union of two lovers

        in marriage

is like the first fruit

     ....of the first flower

        ....of that seed.

Marriage is a word uttered
by four lips
proclaiming the heart a throne....
....Love a king....
....and fidelity a crown.
It is the beginning
of that magic vibration....
....that carries the lovers
from the world of weights and measures....
....into the world of dreams
....and revelations.

.... it is that brief moment
which unfolds before the soul
the chronicles of time,
    and reveals to the eyes
    .... the deeds of the night
        .... and the works of conscience.
    It opens Eternity's secrets of the future.

It is the first flame
that lights up the inner domain
of the heart....
....it is the first magic note
plucked on the silver string
of the heart....

Marriage begins
    with the first look
    ....and the first kiss.
The first look
    between lover and beloved
divides the intoxication of Life....
    ....from the awakening.

Oh seekers....
Love is Truth
....beseeching Truth....
and your Truth in seeking
....and receiving
....and protecting Love
shall determine its behavior.

Life without Love
is like a tree without blossoms
and fruit....
....and Love without Beauty
is like flowers without scent
and fruits without seeds.

Love is the gentle smile
upon the lips of beauty.
       When youth overtakes love....
he forgets his toil....
....and his whole life becomes
a reality....
....of sweet dreams.

Love is the lover's eyes

....and the spirit's wine

....and the heart's nourishment.

Love is a rose.

Its heart opens at dawn

and the virgin kisses the blossom

....and places it

upon her breast.

....and I shall be

until the end of days.

There is no ending to my existence.

For the human soul is but a part

of a burning torch....

....which God separated from Himself

at Creation.

Thus my soul and your soul

are one....

....and we are one with God.

Like you, I have been here
since the beginning....

May 11, 1975

To Mom
    With Love
        Nola
May you have
many more
    Mother's Days.

The Beauty of Life

By Kahlil Gibran

Author of *The Prophet*

Selected by Dean Walley

Illustrated by Fred Klemushin

♛ Hallmark Crown Editions